眠れない星
the sleepless planet

多言語 俳句アンソロジー

haiku
from many parts
of the planet

現代俳句協会 国際部
the international section
modern haiku association

[The International Section]
Toshio Kimura (Chair)
Kayo Baba; Yoshiko Fukushima;
Toshie Tai; Hiroko Takahashi; Mitsuru Tamagawa
[Cover painting: Kayo Baba]

the sleepless planet
haiku from many parts of the planet

Edited by Toshio Kimura
Translated by Toshio Kimura and David Burleigh
(Except as noted in the texts)

ⓒ 2018 The International Section,
Modern Haiku Association
Kairaku Build. 7F 6-5-4 Sotokanda Chiyoda-ku
Tokyo JAPAN 101-0021
[gendaihaiku@bc.wakwak.com]

Published by Shichigatsu-do
2-26-6 Matsubara Setagaya-ku
Tokyo JAPAN 156-0043

All rights reserved Printed in Tokyo Japan
ISBN978-4-87944-318-2 C0092

眠れない星

the sleepless planet

---

haiku
from many parts
of the planet

眠れない星 the sleepless planet

世界の俳句と多様性	木村聡雄		7
Diversity:			
Haiku in the World	Toshio KIMURA		10
秋尾敏	Bin AKIO	Japan	14
ジャン・アントニーニ	Jean ANTONNI	France	16
馬場佳世	Kayo BABA	Japan	18
ジャニク・ベロー	Janick BELLEAU	Canada	20
デイヴィッド・バーレィ	David BURLEIGH	U.K./Japan	22
マリウス・ケラル	Marius CHELARU	Romania	24
デイヴィッド・コップ	David COBB	U.K.	26
董振華	DONG Zhen Hua	China/Japan	28
マイケル・フェスラー	Michael FESSLER	U.S./Japan	30
福島芳子	Yoshiko FUKUSHIMA	Japan	32
リチャード・ギルバート	Richard GILBERT	U.S./Japan	34
リー・ガーガ	Lee GURGA	U.S.	36
播磨穹鷹	Kyūō HARIMA	Japan	38
今泉康弘	Yasuhiro IMAIZUMI	Japan	40
ジム・ケイシャン	Jim KACIAN	U.S.	42
アラン・ケルヴェルヌ	Alain KERVERN	France	44
木村聡雄	Toshio KIMURA	Japan	46
セルゲイ・クルバトフ	Sergiy KURBATOV	Ukraine	48
桑原三郎	Saburō KUWABARA	Japan	50
デイヴィッド・G・ラヌー	David G. LANOUE	U.S.	52
ポール・m.	paul m.	U.S.	54
松田ひろむ	Hiromu MATSUDA	Japan	56

パウル・メルケン	Paul MERCKEN	Netherlands	58
レナード・D・ムーア	Lenard D. MOORE	U.S.	60
トニ・ピッチーニ	Toni PICCINI	Italy	62
フィリップ・ローランド	Philip ROWLAND	U.K./Japan	64
ケシャブ・シグデル	Keshab SIGDEL	Nepal	66
田井淑江	Toshie TAI	Japan	68
玉川満	Mitsuru TAMAGAWA	Japan	70
高橋比呂子	Hiroko TAKAHASHI	Japan	72
ディートマー・タフナー	Dietmar TAUCHNER	Austria	74
チャールズ・トランブル	Charles TRUMBULL	U.S.	76
筑紫磐井	Bansei TSUKUSHI	Japan	78
ヘルマン・ファン=ロンパイ	Herman VAN ROMPUY	Belgium	80
マイケル・ディラン・ウェルチ	Michael Dylan WELCH	U.S./U.K.	82
山﨑十生	Jussei YAMAZAKI	Japan	84

世界の俳句と多様性

木村聡雄

　この俳句アンソロジーは、現代俳句協会の創立70周年と連動する形で、編集出版されたものである。協会創設は1947年のことであるが、終戦後まもなくの国内外の混乱の時代にあって、先人たちは俳句という詩の結集を目指したのであった。その意思は時代を越えて、世界各地の俳句の結集という進化形となってここに受け継がれていると言えるだろう。

　協会創設当時、俳句形式がこれほど世界へと広まってゆこうとは誰一人として想像さえしなかったに違いない。明治時代に俳句が初めて海外に伝えられてから、海外の各国の言語においてもなおこの形式が優れた詩形であることが認識され、それぞれの言葉で広く綴られるようになったのは主に戦後のことであった。そう考えると、我が国の現代俳句協会の70年の歴史とほぼ重なる歳月、地球の各地で俳句形式追及の試行錯誤が続けられてきたと言えるのである。日本と海外それぞれにおいて、俳句の伝統を尊重しつつも、そこに現代の詩としての存在意義を見出そうという作句努力が続けられてきた。その到達点のひとつがここに凝縮されている。

　本詞華集に参加した俳人たちは各国の第一線で活躍中の方々だが、皆、国際部とさまざまな点で関わりのある仲間たちでもある。したがって本書はいわばわれわれの活動記録でもあり、国際部の世界的広がりの一端を示すものと期待している。英語

圏の俳句詩人たちの間では、〈Gendai Haiku〉という英語表現は文字通り「現代的な俳句」すなわち「伝統を超える俳句」を指す英語表現となりつつあることも、わが国際部の活動が世界に与えた影響のひとつであると考えている。

　ここに見られる世界の俳句の広がりは、単に空間的・距離的な隔たりを示すだけではない。表現精神そのもの広がりでもある。表された主題とその手法は多岐にわたっているが、あるものは現代における伝統性を追求し、またあるものは前衛的ですらある。たとえば一般的な外国語俳句の三行書きに対して、近年海外で人気となっている一行の作品がある。これは言うまでもなく、日本の俳句のほとんどが一行で書かれていることに由来する。

　　　山に雲われ実在に届かずに　　　　　　　　ジム・ケイシャン

あるいは、日本の戦後の四行前後の多行書きを上回る実験的多行作品もみられる。

死
を
あらしめよ

この
泉
のごと

つるべ落としの
夜
となる　　　　　　　　　　　フィリップ・ローランド

　　　　　　　　（和訳：木村聡雄）〈二句とも〉

　これらの景色の多様性とは、本来、日本の現代俳句の歴史の多面性そのものでもあったはずである。思い起こせば、明治時代の正岡子規のもう一人の弟子、河東碧梧桐とその流れの俳人たちが目指した新傾向俳句から自由律、あるいは新興俳句、さらには戦後の革新派の俳句の多様さがすぐに浮かんでくるだろう。
　本書の作品群に見られるように二十一世紀の世界の俳句は、もはや日本の古典的俳句を模倣する状況を通り過ぎて、すでに意識的な自己表現の段階へと発展しつつある。その点で多様性を志向するかつての俳句精神は海外に引き継がれて発展しつつあると捉えることもできるのではないだろうか。

　この企画は実際のところ数年前から開始されたものであるが、編集の都合により発行までに思いのほか長い時間がかかってしまった。お待ちいただいた関係の皆様の忍耐に心よりお礼申しあげたい。

〔木村聡雄：現代俳句協会国際部長〕

Diversity: Haiku in the World

Toshio Kimura

This haiku anthology is published in conjunction with the 70th anniversary of the founding of the Gendai Haiku Kyōkai, or Modern Haiku Association, which was set up in 1947. It was a time of hardship and disorder just after the war, and haiku poets then wished to join together to reaffirm the haiku form. Their spirits are reflected here in a new kind of joining together of haiku written across the planet.

When the Association was founded, no one would have expected that haiku would become so popular around the world. Yet since being introduced to the western world in the Meiji era, the haiku has been recognized as an outstanding poetic form even in languages other than Japanese. It was mainly after the war that haiku came to be written in other languages widely, that is to say, those years of the development of haiku in many parts of the world and the history of the Association overlapped each other. Respecting its tradition, poets around the world have tried to discover new value in haiku as a modern poetic form.

The poets appearing in this anthology are truly active in the vanguard of their respective countries, yet also related to the International Section of the Association, and this in turn shows the spread of the group's activities. Through its active engagement, the Japanese word "*gendai*" has come to mean "modern" or "non-traditional" even in English.

The expansion of haiku in the world reveals itself not only in terms of its spatial reach, but also in the variety of its means of expression. The themes and styles are wide-ranging: while some are traditional, others are distinctly avant-garde. There are one-line haiku, which have become popular:

clouds over mountains i can't reach what's real

Jim Kacian

and experimental ones as much as nine lines long:

let
death
be

like
this
well

bucket
night
fall

Philip Rowland

This diversity has been seen before in the history of Japanese haiku: one of the disciples of Shiki Masaoka, Hekigotō Kawahigashi (1873-1936), and his followers created *Shin-Keikō* (New-Trend) haiku, and then *Jiyūritsu* (Free-Style) haiku; we can also recall *Shinkō* (New-Rising) haiku before and during the war, and Avant-garde haiku after the war.

As shown in this anthology, haiku outside Japan has already passed the time when it merely imitated the style of the Japanese original, and has developed to a new stage, where self-expression is consciously sought. The haiku spirits that seek for diversity can be said to have succeeded in haiku around the world.

This project started a few years ago and took some time to complete for various reasons. I would like to express my gratitude to everyone concerned for their kind patience.

Toshio Kimura:
Chair of the International Section,
Gendai Haiku Kyōkai / Modern Haiku Association

秋尾　敏（日本）

傷つけてきた万象に種を撒く

急ぐなよ葡萄は一粒ずつ青い

秒針に冬の重さが少しずつ

冬の川記憶の川に流れこむ

学校の兎前歯を光らせる

Bin Akio (Japan)

I sow the universe
that has been damaged
with seeds

Do not hurry,
each one of the grapes
green

Onto the second hands
the weight of winter
little by little

A wintry river
flowing into
a river of memory

A school rabbit
its front teeth
gleaming

ジャン・アントニーニ（フランス）

碧空
旅立った女性の　　眼
裸木に

子規の句から
作句ふたたび
夏終わる

牛鳴かぬ
この静寂なく
読み書きできたか

空に刻む
無 雲 風 鳥 無
三行目なし

野を行きて
草の葉思いつつ
戻る

Jean Antonini (France)

Grand ciel bleu
D'une femme disparue   les yeux
sur un arbre nu

Bright blue sky
Of a departed woman   the eyes
on a bare tree

Quelques lignes de Shiki
me redonnent le goût d'écrire
Fin de l'été

Some lines from Shiki
give me back the taste for writing
Summer's end

Le silence des vaches
Pourrais-je écrire ? parler ?
sans ce silence-là

The silence of cows
Could I write ? speak ?
without that silence

Gravé dans le ciel
rien nuages air oiseaux rien
pas de ligne 3

Etched on the sky
nothing clouds air birds nothing
no line 3

Traverser le pré
en pensant à chaque brin d'herbe
et revenir

To cross the field
thinking about each blade of grass
and to come back

(English translation : Michael O'dea)

馬場　佳世　（日本）

手にとまる螢の軽さ何祈らむ

空映す海みづ色の魚満ちる

月面の浮き伏しあらわ霜の声

地球が昇る迷いの渦が揺れ昇る

工場夜景は銀河を隠し眠らざる

Kayo Baba (Japan)

A weightless firefly
stopped on my hand—
what should I pray for?

The sea reflecting the sky
filled with fish
of water colours

Clearly up and down
on the surface of the moon—
whispers of frost

The Earth rises—
the vortex of delusions
wavering on it

A factory lit up—
hiding the galaxy
without sleeping

ジャニク・ベロー（カナダ）

路傍
その日蔭生まれの
野の花よ

田舎宿—
窓からは草を食むもの
雨に

書を読めば
膝には日差し
波砕ける

カーテンより
闇夜のきざし
やがて...夜明け

冬の日曜
カシミア、サテンの隙間
女の香水

Janick Belleau (Canada)

sur la chaussée
sa naissance à l'ombre
la fleur sauvage

on the road
its birth in the shade
the wild flower

hôtel champêtre—
de la fenêtre les voir paître
sous la pluie

country hotel—
from the window to see them graze
under the rain

pause lecture
le soleil sur mes genoux
les vagues s'agitent

reading time
the sun on my knees
waves are crashing

le rideau laisse filtrer
un soupçon de nuit noire
peu à peu ... l'aurore

the curtain lets in
a hint of dark night
gradually... dawn

dimanche d'hiver
entre cachemire et satin
un parfum de femme

winter Sunday
between cashmere and satin
a woman's perfume

デイヴィッド・バーレィ（イギリス／日本）

もう一通が
返信を待ち—
竹そびゆ

伝言として
不在者に
黄葉摘めり

砂丘にて
海見るひとに
虹すこし

横顔の王
象牙の耳に
鳥鳴かず

暗闇に花—
色の不在という
不思議

David Burleigh (U.K./Japan)

Another letter
still waiting for an answer—
the soaring bamboo

To leave a message
for someone who is absent
pick a yellow leaf

Over the sand dunes
where a man stares out to sea
part of a rainbow

The king in profile –
no birdsong ever reaches
his ivory ear

Flowers in the dark:
the absence of colour is
a kind of wonder

マリウス・ケラル（ルーマニア）

霧の道—
鹿の目は
まだ泣いている

魚の眼から太陽を
呑む湖や—
夏

陽溜まりの
黒犬—
凍てる窓辺にて

広島と福島
の歳月
放射線煙る

鴨川は
古舟のさえぎる
月明かり

Marius Chelaru (Romania)

șosea în ceață —
ochii căprioarei încă
mai lăcrimează

Lacul înghite
soarele prin ochiul
peștelui— vară

Un câine negru
în soarele roșu—
pe geamul brumat

anii dintre
Hiroshima și Fukushima
fum radioactiv

pe râul Kamo
canoea veche taie
lumina lunii

foggy road—
deer's eyes
still weeping

the lake swallows
the sun through the eye
of the fish—summer

a black dog
in the red sun—
on the frosted window

years between
Hiroshima and Fukushima
radioactive smoke

on the Kamo river
the old canoe cuts
the moonlight

デイヴィッド・コッブ（イギリス）

地震揺れ
役場の庭師
鍬を引く

スイカ
その皮に刻まれた
名はキーツ

桜桃苦し
黒歌鳥とわれ
種を吐く

半分ほど
姿を見せて
雪のカササギ

報われぬ愛の
歌また
春八重むぐら

David Cobb (U.K.)

earthquake tremor
the municipal gardener
draws back his hoe

water melon
the name of Keats
cut in its rind

bitter cherries
blackbirds and myself
spitting pips

no more than
half itself
the magpie in snow

that song again
of unrequited love
goose grass in spring

董　振華（中国／日本）

葉桜や車窓を装飾的な通過

　　　　　　　　　　　　櫻花散落新葉萌、株株裝飾車窗景

掌紋に消えゆく春の合言葉

　　　　　　　　　　　　春日約定猶在耳、擊掌余音紋中逝

秋落日伴舞のごと白鷺一羽

　　　　　　　　　　　　落日孤鷺相伴舞、秋景長天交輝映

冬の夜の全景として月一輪

　　　　　　　　　　　　冬夜漫漫心露重、一輪明月映全景

静寂に唯一のかたち飛雪かな

　　　　　　　　　　　　鳥藏人隱歸靜寂、唯見飛雪飄蒼宇

Dong Zhen Hua (China/Japan)

Cherry tree in leaf
passing decoratively
beyond the train window

In the lines on my palm
a spring password
vanishes

Autumnal sunset
like a dance partner
— a white eagle

For the entire view
on a wintry night—
a single moon

In all the silence
the only shape—
a flying snowflake

マイケル・フェスラー（アメリカ／日本）

水光り
落書きの色
花不明

これまではよし
真夜中の
一分後

秋の暮
暗き二地点
つなぐ橋

一昨日より
昨日より
今日

「そう言えば」―
もとの話に
戻らぬ彼女

Michael Fessler (U.S./Japan)

the shining water
the colors of graffiti
the missing flowers

so far so good
one minute
after midnight

autumn dusk
a bridge connecting
two dark places

today more
than yesterday than
the day before

"By the way"—
and she never got
back to the point

福島　芳子（日本）

ドナウ川に掛かる鎖橋月に向かう

マッターホルン南北に切れ雪風飛ぶ

白夜明け孔雀時計覚め冬日差す

クリムトの接吻絵眩し金箔秋

ラムセス像古代のにおいや秋惜しむ

Yoshiko Fukushima (Japan)

Hanging over the Danube
the Chain Bridge
heading straight for the moon

Matterhorn
cut into the north and the south
—a snow wind flying

Midnight sun passed—
a peacock clock wakes up
pointing to the winter sun

The Kiss by Klimt
dazzling
—gold foil in autumn

Statue of Ramesses II
smell of ancient times—
mourning the autumn

リチャード・ギルバート（アメリカ／日本）

セム戦争
オリーブ無傷―砂漠は
君の肌の味

星
いつもの夜
一曲がまた一曲を

それから　　　　裸身
普段の　　　　　沈黙
恐れの　　　　　狭間に

どこまでも走り続け
悲劇の後の
春

それについては浜辺に木々のわきの二つの瞬間その隙間には

Richard Gilbert (U.S./Japan)

semite war
unharmed olives — the desert
tastes your skin

stars
in the natural night
one song threads another

then   nude
normal   silence
between   fears

running forever
spring after
tragedy

about it on the beach by the trees two moments between that is

リー・ガーガ（アメリカ）

ポテトチップその他八百万の神々よ

青揚羽心理の隅に潜むもの

腕いっぱいの飾り
　　　　　　でもひとりぼっちの
　　　雪片

丘の墓地
あの世に触れる
我が舌で

おんどり鳴く
老兵二人
酒場にて

(Japanese translation by Hiroko Schatz)

Lee Gurga (U.S.)

potato chips and other gods

blue swallowtail corner of the psyche

armsful of bangles
                but lonely
      snowflakes

hilltop cemetery
touching another world
with my tongue

rooster crowing
two old soldiers
at the bar

播磨　穹鷹（日本）

無意識に掻き回されし暑さかな

酷暑なり言葉探しておりにけり

誰が作ったか人に生まれて　裸

ペリカンも汚れて人間も汚れて

裸婦が背伸びしているリラの冷え

Kyūō Harima (Japan)

being stirred around
unconsciously—
the heat

the intense heat—
searching
for a word for my haiku

who made me?
born as a man
—naked

pelicans
getting dirty
humans beings too

A nude woman
stretching—
chill in the lilac season

今泉　康弘（日本）

血まみれのものの一つや雪だるま

原爆の図に妹の裸かな

方舟に乗り遅れたり秋刀魚焼く

死者の書やかくまでつちのふるなかに

睡蓮の花から花へ神の息

Yasuhiro Imaizumi (Japan)

one
of bloody things:
a snowman

in the A-bomb picture
— my sister's
naked body

late for the ark
—grilling
sauries

Book of the Dead—
In such
hard-falling dirt

from a lotus flower
to another
—God's breath

ジム・ケイシャン（アメリカ）

神よりも古し
地獄への
入口は

浅瀬行く
どちらの岸も
遠き一瞬

山に雲われ実在に届かずに

つながりのすべてはどこか妄想へ

鞭一本もちいず馬に鞭 悟り

Jim Kacian (U.S.)

older than god
the cave mouth
to hell

fording the river
the moment closer
to neither bank

clouds over mountains i can't reach what's real

all the links go somewhere paranoid

beating a horse with no stick satori

アラン・ケルヴェルヌ（フランス）

空黒し
傷ついた海の
声に重く

岩礁
夜を研ぎつつ
死者に語らせよ

千の嵐
千の積もりし夢
万の潮

蝶迷う
潮と風との
白の啓示

大嵐
真白きサンザシ
海歩く

Alain Kervern (France)

L'air est noir
chargé des appels
de l'océan blessé

Les récifs
affûtent la nuit
qui fait parler les morts

Mille tempêtes
mille rêves ensablés
dix mille marées

Un papillon s'égare
oracle blanc
des marées et des vents

L'orage en majesté
un prunellier tout blanc
marche sur les eaux

Black is the air
heavy with the calls
of the wounded ocean

The reefs
whetting the night
that gives tongue to the dead

One thousand tempests
one thousand silted up dreams
ten thousand tides

A stray butterfly
white oracle
of tides and winds

The magnificent storm
a blackthorn entirely white
walks on the waters

木村　聡雄（日本）

ドーナツをわが王冠と思えど夏

夢にて詠める句よ畏怖だけを持ち帰る

月蝕やあの遁走の句を嘆く

春を告げてもマストドンは動かない

ニャーニャーヴァイオリン月蹴ってモー

Toshio Kimura (Japan)

thinking of a doughnut
as my crown—
summer, though

I made a haiku
in my dream – only the awe
left over from it

a lunar eclipse ——
I regret a haiku
that eluded me

even when told it's spring,
the mastodon
stays still

mew mew violin,
kicking the moon
and there goes moo

セルゲイ・クルバトフ（ウクライナ）

夕陽より
地平へと
影落ち行けり

黄昏は
見たこともない
詩をつかめ

コマ送り―
閃光いくつ
嵐前

春気分―
花々に
風まとわれば

暦―
その新たな日付の
裏の生

Sergiy Kurbatov (Ukraine)

от заката
до самого горизонта
уходят тени

под вечер
незнакомые стихи
ловлю на слове

стоп-кадр —
до начала грозы
пара вспышек

духи весны —
путается в лепестках
тёплый ветер

календарь —
жизнь с обратной стороны
новой даты

from sunset
to the horizon
shadows are falling

at twilight
catching snaps
of unfamiliar verse

freeze-frame —
a few flashes
before the storm

spring spirits —
the wind is tangled
in the blossoms

calendar —
the life on the back side
of a new date

(English translation by Tatiana Nekriach)

桑原　三郎（日本）

永き日の欠伸は嚙まず殺さずに

どの道も自宅へつづく夏の月

夕焼けや日本中に人がゐて

幽霊は肩のちからを抜いてくる

新涼や指紋うすれし指を嗅ぐ

Saburō Kuwabara (Japan)

On a long day
I neither stifle
nor kill my yawns

Every street
leads home
—summer moon

Sunset—
all over Japan
there are people

A ghost:
haunting
in a relaxed manner

Fresh coolness—
smelling my fingers
on which the prints have faded

デイヴィッド・G・ラヌー（アメリカ）

画面消え
まだ息のある
潰したユスリカ

水たまりに円形
雨粒
死すところ

別の踊り子
我に下着を売り
スイカズラ

蛇と聞き
さらにそろりと
わが歩み

花咲く街を
ゆったり走る
二輪の棺

David G. Lanoue (U.S.)

still twitching
as the screen goes dark
my broken gnat

circles on puddles
where raindrops
go to die

another stripper
sells me her panties
honeysuckle

talk of snakes
I tread
more softly

cruising through
a city of flowers
two wheeled coffin

ポール・m．(アメリカ)

初アイリス
原子と原子
その距離は

流星夜
鴉の眼玉
光へと

冬深し
犬を呼ぶのに
用いる名

詩人から
一行借りて
春の雨

水仙の芽－
この年月を
会計士

paul m. (U.S.)

first iris
the distance
between atoms

night of the comet
the eye of a crow
turns to the light

deep winter
the name I use
to call the dog

a line borrowed
from another poet
spring rain

daffodil shoots—
all these years
as an accountant

松田ひろむ （日本）

鬼灯市や子規に恋の句あればなあ

西銀座風鈴売が風売る

涙そうそう墓標の数の風薫る
(なだ)

人ノ上ニ人ヲ作ラズ葡萄棚

お茶碗を洗う小流れ天の川

Hiromu Matsuda (Japan)

Chinese-lantern plant fair
I wish
Shiki had written love haiku

in Nishi-Ginza town
a wind-bell seller
sells wind

tears flowing—
winds redolent of the number
of grave posts

heaven does not create a man
above another man—
a grapevine trellis

washing my rice bowl
in a stream—
the Milky Way

パウル・メルケン（オランダ）

朝の霧―
錆びたレールに
突然ポピー

滝しぶき
一気に跳んで
泡のなか

パン屋橋あたり
通りに埠頭に
笛の音

霜の野は
密かに霞み
景うつろ

最期の味は
苦扁桃か
ドクゼリか

Paul Mercken (Netherlands)

mistige morgen —
plots tussen de roestige rails
een bed klaprozen

klater waterval
en stort je met groot geweld
in je bruisend bad

bij de bakkersbrug
tuimelt over straat en werf
een fluitmelodie

berijmde velden
ongemerkt lossen ze op
in vage verten

de smaak van de dood
bittere amandelen
of dollekervel

misty morning —
suddenly between the rusty rails
a bed of poppies

splatter waterfall
and throw yourself with great force
into your seething bath

near the bakers bridge
over street and wharf tumbles
a flute melody

frosted fields
unnoticed they dissolve
into vague vistas

the taste of death
bitter almonds
or water hemlock

レナード・D・ムーア（アメリカ）

ジャズ響く
浮世絵店の
肌寒し

列車の汽笛
町向こうから
秋の風

葬列や
陽に
静かなる綿の花

雨のち虹
故郷へと
わが五十年

彼女には足袋の
白さよ―
空暗し

Lenard D. Moore (U.S.)

jazz
in the Japanese print shop
slight chill

a train whistles
from the other side of town
autumn wind

funeral procession
the stillness of cotton blossoms
in sunlight

rain and rainbow
toward my hometown
my five decades

whiteness
of her *tabi*—
black sky

トニ・ピッチーニ（イタリア）

鴨飛ぶや―
意志とは
どこまでも魔法

葡萄園
風の記憶と
未踏の地

港には聖歌隊―
波が聴く
残響

この不思議なる神といて
辞書
要らず

目に見えぬ龍に
忘却の
記憶なお

Toni Piccini (Italy)

Anatre in volo—
l'infinito fascino
della volontà

Ducks in flight—
the endless enchantment
of the will

Nei vigneti
i ricordi del vento
e terre inesplorate

In the vineyards
the wind's memories
and uncharted territories

Un coro nel porto—
le onde ascoltano
il proprio eco

Choir of the harbor—
the waves listen
to their echo

Con un Dio straniero
non ho bisogno
di dizionari

With this strange God
I have no need
of a dictionary

Il Drago Invisible
custodisce la memoria
ora dimenticata

The Invisible Dragon
preserves a memory
now forgotten

フィリップ・ローランド（イギリス／日本）

曲前の摩擦音
私ではない人
の音

空　電線　これほど　電線　青く　電線

まばゆい秋の昼―
突然鳥の歌
鞄から

死
を
あらしめよ

この
井戸
のごと

つるべ落としの
夜
となる

木の葉
わが幼年時代の
底に残し

Philip Rowland (U.K./Japan)

in the hush before music
the music of who
I am not

sky wires so wires blue wires

bright autumn noon –
a sudden chorus of birds from inside
a briefcase

let
death
be

like
this
well

bucket
night
fall

leaf I leave
on the floor of
my childhood

ケシャブ・シグデル（ネパール）

暗き夜
地上に星をもたらす
蛍

何という陶酔
現実を飛ぶ
かの芋虫

うら若き日
葉の上になぜ
この露が

空腹よ
山羊を屠りて
神への供物

妻求めれば
いかなる苦難も
独身者

Keshab Sigdel (Nepal)

अमवस्यामा
धर्तीमा तारा झार्छ
जुनकिरीले

In the dark night
They bring the stars to the earth
The fireflies

कस्तो मात हो
विषमामै उड्छ, त्यो
झुसिलकिरा

What intoxication
Flies in the reality
That caterpillar

चढेपछि वैंश
किन बस्छ पातमा
शितको थोपा

In the utmost youthfulness
Why it sits on the leaf
The dew drop

भोकको आगो
बलिचढेका बोक्रा
ईश्वर पूजा

Hunger instinct
Makes the goats ready for sacrifice
A God's offering

श्रीमती खोज्न
के पो गरेन होला
बाल ब्रम्हचारी

In search of a wife
Tried hard every possibility
This celibate

田井　淑江（日本）

ほんとうは真っ白が好き寒椿

浮世絵の余白のゆらぎ春浅し

流氷の影より空海現れて

凍蝶の記憶うすれてゆく目覚め

森羅万象仄かに揺れて合歓の花

Toshie Tai (Japan)

to tell the truth I like
pure white color—
camellia in winter

flickering
blank of an ukiyo-e print
—early spring

behind drifting ice
appears
priest Kūkai

Memory of frozen butterfly
fades away
—waking

All things in the universe
faintly trembling—
silk tree flowers

玉川　満（日本）

ミシンの針が
折れる不安
振り子の音
なりやまず

ああ
岸の喜び
割れてゆく
岩の恍惚

めまいの夜は
足の爪ばかり
伸びている

島に流され

王手を詰めぬ
あな、君子

塩も汚れて
母なる海が
滅びる
あした

Mitsuru Tamagawa (Japan)

needle of a sewing machine
may break
sound of a pendulum clock
never stops

ah,
coast in joy;
rock in ecstasy
cracking

dizzy at night
only toenails
growing

banished to an island

not trying to check
ah, a fine gentleman

salt also soiled
the mother ocean
perished
tomorrow

高橋　比呂子（日本）

てのひらで故郷こわれし桔梗かな

豌豆のいちからはじまるはなしかな

百日紅すこしよごれて憎きたり

金魚二匹戦争を知らざりき

雷雲をひきよせている調律師

Hiroko Takahashi (Japan)

on my palm
my home village deserted—
Japanese bellflowers

tales of green peas
starting
from the beginning

crepe myrtle
getting dirty a little—
a priest appeared

two goldfishes
not knowing
any war

drawing
thunder clouds
a piano tuner

ディートマー・タフナー（オーストリア）

野の奥の
秘密へ向かう
ひまわりよ

冬の朝
目覚めればこの夢なる
未来

わが窓の向こう未知へと至る窓

新しきラジオ
我らの原初の
音が

夜の風
恐れとは
未来から来たる

Dietmar Tauchner (Austria)

Tiefes Feld
Sonnenblumen wenden sich
dem Geheimnis zu

deep field
sunflowers facing
the secret

Wintermorgen
ich erwache in der Zukunft
meines Traums

winter morning
i wake up in the future
of my dream

hinter meinem Fenster ein Fenster ins Unbekannte

    beyond my window a window to the unknown

neues Radio
Rauschen
unseres Ursprungs

new radio
noise
of our origin

Nachtwind
Furcht hergeleitet
aus der Zukunft

night wind
fear derives
from the future

チャールズ・トランブル（アメリカ）

元旦や―
猫啼く出るたび
入るたび

タンポポ野原
白髪の男
独り言

食卓に
季節外れの花
初キッス

三色菫　われら微笑み返す

彼のその関節炎の手をもて　盆栽

Charles Trumbull (U.S.)

New Year's—
the cat yowls to go out,
to come in

field of dandelions
a gray-haired man
talks to himself

the table filled
with out-of-season flowers
first kiss

pansies   we smile back

with his arthritic hands   bonsai

筑紫　磐井（日本）

犬を飼ふ　飼ふたびに死ぬ　犬を飼ふ

ひばり揚がり世は面白きこともなし

欲望が輝いてゐた戦後とは

人はみな遺影のために微笑むか

秋風や蝋石で書く詩のごとし

Bansei Tsukushi (Japan)

having a dog
it dies whenever I have it—
having a dog

lark climbs into the sky—
nothing interesting
in this world

postwar period—
when desires
gleam

every one
smiles
for his memorial photo

autumn wind—
like a poem
written in pagodite

ヘルマン・ファン＝ロンパイ（ベルギー）

海静か
老詩人の声
聴く椿

陽を海を
星を見るもの
和を愛す

秋の陽に
積もる枯れ葉の
そのねじれ

青海のうねり
星の輪
とこしえに

友情の奇跡
同じ青空
日また星

Herman Van Rompuy (Belgium)

The sea is silent
old poet speaks softly
even camellias listen.

Who looks at the sun,
at the sea, at the stars
loves peace.

In the autumn sun
a heap of dried leaves lies
curled and contorted.

A wreath made of stars
surging on a blue sea
united forever.

Friendship miracle
A rising sun, shining stars
in the same blue sky.

マイケル・ディラン・ウェルチ（アメリカ／イギリス）

春の雷—
砦の壁に
花の影

日除け広げて—
日陰のみ
カフェの賑やかさ

初霜や...
靴は
そのまま玄関に

巣立ちゆく
娘の眼には
冬の空

引越や...
目に焼き付ける
一家の住まい

Michael Dylan Welch (U.S./U.K.)

spring lightning—
a flower's shadow
against the fortress wall

unfurled awning—
the café crowded
only in the shade

first frost . . .
a pair of shoes
left at the door

leaving home . . .
winter sky
in my daughter's eyes

moving . . .
our last view
of the family homestead

山﨑　十生（日本）

せっけんを洗うことから原発忌

陽炎の全身触手なりしかな

消えるのはマイナスなどではないぞ露

削げるだけ削いで色なき風となる

霜柱減ずる力蓄へる

Jussei Yamazaki (Japan)

I wash soap first
—the anniversary of
the nuclear power plant accident

heat haze
its whole body:
a feeler

even being gone
never useless
—dewdrops

cutting off
as possible
to be a colorless wind

frost columns—
saving power
to diminish

〔現代俳句協会　国際部〕
木村聡雄（部長）
馬場佳世、福島芳子、
田井淑江、高橋比呂子、玉川満
［表紙画　馬場佳世］

眠れない星
多言語 俳句アンソロジー

編集　　木村聡雄
翻訳　　木村聡雄、デイヴィッド・バーレィ
　　　　（本文に示した箇所を除く）

発行日　2018年5月20日
発行者　現代俳句協会 国際部
　　　　101-0021 東京都千代田区外神田 6-5-4 偕楽ビル 7 階
　　　　gendaihaiku@bc.wakwak.com

発売元　七月堂
　　　　156-0043 東京都世田谷区松原 2-26-6

ISBN　978-4-87944-318-2　C0092